Winning
The Office
Leasing Game©

Winning
The Office
Leasing Game©

Essential Strategies for Negotiating Your Office Lease Like an Expert

Karen Warner

VISION
Publications

Turning Your Business Vision into Reality

www.moveyouroffice.com

Winning the Office Leasing Game©: Essential Strategies for Negotiating Your Office Lease Like an Expert

Contents

1 | Understanding the Office Leasing Process

Leasing office space is among the highest expenses a business incurs, second only to the cost of salaries and wages. It can also be a time-consuming and stressful process. Being organized and prepared will give your company an advantage, enabling you to move into your preferred location at competitive terms.

The steps involved in the office leasing process are outlined below. The following chapters provide details to help you negotiate the best possible terms for your office lease.

Needs Analysis - Define your basic requirements for office space.

- Calculate the amount of square footage your business will need.

- Determine the type of building that best suits your business and brand.

- Choose your preferred location.

- Consider employee needs, services, and amenities.

Market Research - Study market conditions and locate available property vacancies.

- Conduct a thorough market survey of available properties meeting your requirements or obtain a list of available properties from your commercial real estate agent.

- Reduce the list of properties by excluding any that are unsuitable.

Tour Properties - Complete site visits for each of the properties that meet your facility requirements.

- Schedule a property tour for each of the remaining facilities.

- Tour properties, recording specific features and notes for each site.

- If necessary, revisit specific properties to gather additional information.

Establish a Short List - Narrow your list of properties to the top few that are the most desirable.

- Compare property characteristics, including size, cost, location and image.

- Identify the two or three properties that best meet your criteria.

Preliminary Space Planning - Define any modifications that will be required to make each space ideal for your business.

- Engage an architect to create a preliminary space plan for each of your top two or three building alternatives.

- Determine the general type and scope of the changes your business requires for each property.

- Establish the estimated cost and duration of construction and remodeling.

Requests for Proposal (RFPs) - Encourage competition between landlords with a detailed RFP.

- Prepare and distribute Requests for Proposal (RFPs) to the landlords of your top two or three building choices.

- Receive RFP responses from landlords.

Select a Building or Space - Determine which space is your first choice.

- Prepare an objective analysis to evaluate the RFP responses received.

- Based on the RFP analysis and the preliminary space plans, determine which space would be the best alternative for your business.

Letter of Intent - Prepare a Letter of Intent outlining your preferred lease terms.

- Submit a Letter of Intent to the landlord of your selected property.

- Negotiate Letter of Intent terms with landlord.

Review Lease and Negotiate Terms - Finalize lease document.

- Request a draft lease from the landlord.

- Review the lease with your commercial real estate agent, the decision maker(s) from your company and your real estate attorney.

- Submit a redlined lease with your requested changes to landlord.

- Further negotiate lease terms, if required, until they are acceptable to all parties.

Space Planning - Complete a formal space plan and architectural drawings.

- Make any necessary changes to the preliminary space plan.

- Complete detail on finishes, electrical and lighting.

- Confirm construction costs fit within negotiated lease terms and/or your budget.

- Have your architect finalize the space plan and attach it to the lease.

Execute Lease - Complete the leasing process by executing all documentation.

- You and the landlord sign the lease.

- Submit a check for the deposit and first month's rent, if required.

- Original signed documents distributed to all parties to the contract.

Schedule and Manage Remodel/Construction - Manage the tenant improvement process and prepare space for your occupancy.

- Monitor construction progress throughout the build-out period.

- Perform the final walk-through of the remodeled space.

- Apply for and receive a Certificate of Occupancy.

2 | Office Leasing Concepts

There are several concepts that are important to understand as you begin the process of finding and leasing office space.

Understanding Rental Rates and Lease Structure

When considering your budget for rent, it is critical to determine what is included, and what is not included, in the rental rate and what your total monthly and annual cost for office space will be.

There are multiple methods of quoting rental rates – some include janitorial services, utilities, real estate taxes, common area and grounds maintenance; others do not. It is essential to find out what is included in the rental rate and whether there are any associated costs you will be required to pay for over and above the quoted rental rate.

Rental rates are based on the following building operating expense components:

Base Rent – an amount determined by the landlord, which represents the cost and benefit of ownership. The landlord's mortgage payments, equity and return on investment are typical items that fall under this category.

Taxes – property taxes on the building.

Insurance – insurance policy on the building; does not include tenant liability or personal property insurance.

Common Area Maintenance (CAM) – building maintenance, window cleaning, snow removal, parking lot and grounds maintenance, management fees, security and any other general maintenance and/or cleaning fees pertaining to the common areas.

Utilities – gas, electric, water, etc.

Tenant Janitorial and Other Costs – maintenance within a particular suite, such as janitorial services, light bulb replacement, carpet cleaning, painting and repairs.

The type of lease rate structure determines which of these components are paid by the landlord and which are paid by the tenant.

Most commercial leases fall under one of the following structures:

Full Service or Gross Lease

The rental rate for a full service lease includes all of the building operating expense components plus interior maintenance and janitorial service. A full service lease structure is most common in Class A buildings and includes all facets of caring for the building and individual office spaces – even changing the light bulbs.

Modified Gross Lease

Expenses included in a modified gross lease vary by region, but a typical structure includes base rent, property taxes and property insurance, with the tenant paying for some or all utilities and janitorial service.

Net Lease

A net lease usually includes the base rent, insurance and common area maintenance. The tenant is responsible for their pro rate share of property taxes and utilities.

Double Net Lease (NN)

Double net leases include base rent, taxes and common area maintenance. The tenant is responsible for their pro rata share of property taxes, insurance and utilities.

Triple-Net Lease (NNN)

A triple-net lease includes only the base rent component for the property itself. Other building expenses – property taxes, insurance and common area maintenance – are the tenant's responsibility. Tenants under a triple-net lease are also responsible for maintaining everything inside their leased space, including utilities, janitorial service, plumbing and the heating/air conditioning system. Medical, industrial and manufacturing facilities are commonly rented on a triple-net basis.

Building owners use net lease structures, including net, double net and triple net leases, to shift some or all of the lease operating expenses to the tenant.

Typically, under any type of net lease structure, the landlord will pay the building operating expenses as they are incurred and then submit an annual or monthly bill to the tenant for reimbursement.

The True Cost of Leasing Office Space

Determine the total cost of leasing a particular space by adding the estimated costs of any additional services or building operating expenses to the quoted rental rate. This is the dollar amount to use when measuring properties against each other in order to achieve a fair rental rate comparison.

For example, if janitorial services are not included in the rental rate and it is estimated that it will cost approximately $2.00 per square foot for that service on an annual basis, add $2.00 to the annual per-square-foot rental rate for comparison purposes.

Rent	+ Additional Expenses	= Equivalent Rent
$27.50	+ 2.00 (janitorial services)	= 29.50 / sq.ft.

Your commercial real estate agent can assist you in determining a dollar value for additional rental expenses (i.e., common area maintenance, utilities, janitorial services, etc.)

Office Space Load Factor

The load factor refers to the portion of the building's common areas that are attributed to your suite. Common areas include the lobby, restrooms, storage/supply rooms, etc. If you are leasing 10,000 square feet, and the building has a load factor of 17%, your rental rate will be based on square footage of 11,700.

While it may appear that you are paying for more square footage than you are using it usually works out to be a pretty fair way to attribute rent to common spaces. For instance, in a multi-tenant high-rise building, you won't need to build restrooms into the actual space your business uses. The restrooms will instead be in a public area of the building that your business will share with other tenants. Conversely, if you were located in a single-tenant building you would need to rent a large space to accommodate for restrooms, utility closets, etc.

The building owner and their architect determine the building's load factor using the Building Owners and Managers Association (BOMA) Guidelines. If the load factor is higher in a particular building than other buildings you are looking at, the overall rent you pay will be proportionately higher as well.

Measuring Office Space

Following is a summary of the Building Owners and Managers Association (BOMA) Guidelines for defining and measuring office space.[1] The purpose of the Standard Method for Measuring Floor Area in Office Buildings is to permit communication and computation on a clear and understandable basis.

The BOMA Standard has been the generally accepted method for measuring office space for many years.

It should be noted that this standard can and should be used in measuring office space in old as well as new buildings. It is applicable to any architectural design or type of construction.

Usable Area

This method measures the actual occupiable area of a floor or an office suite and is of prime interest to a tenant in evaluating the space offered by a landlord and in allocating the space required to house personnel and furniture. The amount of Usable Area on a multi-tenant floor can vary over the life of a building as corridors expand and contract and as floors are remodeled. Usable Area can be converted to Rentable Area by the use of a conversion factor.

The Usable Area of an office shall be computed by measuring to the finished surface side of the office side of corridor and other permanent walls, to the center of the partitions that separate the office from adjoining Usable Areas, and to the inside finished surface of the dominant portions of the permanent outer building walls. No deduction shall be made for columns and projections necessary to the building.

The Usable Area of a floor shall be equal to the sum of all Usable Areas on that floor.

Rentable Area

This method measures the tenant's pro-rata portion of the entire office floor, excluding elements of the building that penetrate through the floor to areas below. The Rentable Area of a building is fixed for the life of a building and is not affected by changes in corridor sizes and configuration.

This method is therefore recommended for measuring the total income producing area of a building and for use in computing the tenant's pro-rata share of a building for purposes of rent escalation. The Rentable Area of floor area shall be computed by measuring to the inside finished surface of the dominant portions of the permanent outer building walls, excluding any major vertical penetrations of the floor.

No deduction shall be made for columns and projections necessary to the building. The Rentable Area of an office on the floor shall be computed by multiplying the Usable Area of that office by the quotient of the division of the Rentable Area of the floor by the Usable Area of the floor resulting in the R/U Ratio.

$$\text{Rentable Area} \div \text{Usable Area} = \text{R/U Ratio}$$

Load Factor

The Load Factor is the percentage of space on a floor that is not usable, expressed as a percent of Usable Area. It is also known as the Common Area Factor, Add-on Factor or the Loss Factor.

[1]Provided by the Building Owners and Managers Association (BOMA)

3 | Establishing Your Office Space Requirements

Now it is time to think about what type of office space you desire and approximately how many square feet you will need. There are many factors to consider when planning your ideal office space.

What direction is the business headed? Think about your company's potential for growth before you start investigating new locations. For example, if you intend to double your staff soon you'll need significantly more space than you will if you want to grow your business at a more moderate pace.

Remember that most space is leased for the long-term, at least five years or longer. Don't lease a space that you will outgrow within the term of your lease.

Factors to consider:

- Number of employees

- Number of desks, cubicles and/or offices

- The need for warehouse, production or showroom space

- Computers, scanners, copiers and other major office equipment

- Storage space for inventory or files

- Office layout (open concept or traditional layout)

Part of analyzing your office requirement is determining what is important for your business to run efficiently. Brainstorm with the individuals or team involved in the process about what works with your current space. Include a discussion on what features of the current space are not very functional.

At this point, you will also want to consider whether your office plan will be mostly cubicles and open area, or if private offices would be more desirable.

When deciding what type of office space is appropriate, and where you would ideally like to locate, it is helpful to address the following considerations.

Rental Budget

The amount of rent you will pay each month for office space represents the square footage of the space you intend to occupy multiplied by the building's rental rate. Rent is usually quoted per square foot on an annual basis, though in some larger metropolitan areas it is quoted per square foot on a monthly basis.

To determine what the rental rate will be on an annual basis, multiply the quoted rate by the number of square feet if the rent is quoted annually. For rental rates which are quoted on a monthly basis, multiply the quoted rate by the number of square feet and then multiply by 12 to determine the annual rate.

Rent	+ Additional Expenses	=	Equivalent Rent
$27.50	+ 2.00 (janitorial services)	=	29.50 / sq.ft.

Other Expenses

As discussed in the previous chapter, different types of buildings use different methods of quoting rental rates—some include janitorial service, utilities, real estate taxes, common area and grounds maintenance; others do not.

It is essential to determine what is included in the rental rate, and whether there are any associated costs you will be required to pay for over and above the rental cost.

A seemingly inexpensive rental rate that doesn't include any services, can often end up being much more expensive than a higher rental rate that is all inclusive.

Employee Needs

Consider how long of a commute your employees will have. Will you lose any key staff members if you choose to relocate to another side of town? Availability of public transportation and traffic patterns can also play a part in this decision.

Conducting an informal survey of the commuting preferences of the existing staff (particularly among key employees you cannot afford to lose) will give you a picture of where people stand on this issue. The important thing to remember is that it is impossible to please everyone when considering a location change.

Your goal should be to retain as many staff members as possible, while ensuring the availability of new employees, to replace those that may decide to leave.

Amenities

Locating your business near a variety of applicable amenities and services is also important for many businesses.

Employees and customers will appreciate being able to have lunch or meetings at nearby restaurants; out of town visitors will enjoy the convenience of having a hotel near the office.

Parking

Determine if there is adequate parking, or if additional parking will have to be secured at a cost to either the company or employees.

Business Relationships

Are there other businesses in town you need to be in proximity to? Often professional firms prefer to be near their largest clients.

Image

For many businesses it's important to project a certain image to their customers. Your company may prefer an opulent image, or you might prefer to project a low-key, economical image. Consider how your customers will react to the image of both the building you are in, and to your particular office space.

Thoroughly discussing these issues will give you a complete picture of the type of office that specifically meets your needs. Your ideal office may be very narrowly defined, or you may be considering several types of different options.

Calculating Office Space Size

The simplest method of calculating a space size requirement is to base the square footage on the number of employees in your office. Most experts estimate that you will need 200 to 225 square feet per employee.

Number of Employees	Square Footage per Employee	Range of Square Feet Required
27	200	5,400
	225	6,075

Your business may also need extra space if you intend to hold a large amount of inventory or if your business requires a lot of open space.

Make sure your facility's size meets the needs of your employees and customers. For example, a business with executive clients who visit frequently, may need additional vacant offices for the visiting employees to use as a temporary office while they are in town.

Office Space Programming

You can also determine your square footage needs by making a list of each individual space you require and then totaling the square footage of those spaces. This is called an Office Space Program and is often performed and calculated by an architect.

An example of an Office Space Program showing square footage requirements for each office area is shown below.

Area	Square Feet Required	# of Areas	Estimated Square Footage	Amount of Square Feet/Area
Executive Office	250 to 400 sq. ft.	1	325	325
Mid-size Office	150 to 250 sq. ft.	3	200	600
Small Office	100 to 150 sq. ft.	3	125	375
Open Space for Cubicles	60 to 110 sq. ft. per cubicle	20	100	2,000
Reception Area	125 to 300 sq. ft. - Room for 2 to 4 guests	1	200	200
	200 to 300 sq. ft. - Room for 6 to 8 guests	1	300	300
Small Conference Room	150 sq. ft. with seating for 6 people	2	150	300
Large Conference Room	250 sq. ft. with seating for 8 to 10 people	1	400	400
Library	175 to 450 sq. ft. with seating for 4 to 6	0	0	0
File Room	75 to 150 sq. ft. holds 10 to 20 file cabinets	1	125	125
Mail Room	80 to 250 sq. ft.	1	80	80
Work Area	100 to 150 sq. ft.	1	150	150
Lunch Room	200 sq. ft. will accommodate 10 people	1	200	200
Server/Network Room	75 to 150 sq. ft.	1	150	150
Storage Room	100 to 300 sq. ft.	1	125	125
Corridors	Add 15 - 20% for corridors and workflow		20%	971
Total				**6,301**

For additional advice on calculating your square footage needs, consider contacting your industry's trade association. They should be able to provide you with average annual sales per square foot. For example, if the yearly revenue goal for your business is $600,000 and your trade group estimates an average of $150 of sales per square foot, you will need approximately 4,000 square feet of space ($600,000 divided by $150).

Determining space needs is not an exact science. An architect or space planner may be able to help you fit into a space slightly smaller than your original requirement by creating efficiencies in the office layout.

4 | Analyzing Available Spaces

If you haven't done so already, now is a good time to consider hiring a commercial real estate agent. A good agent will provide information on available properties and may also know of some unadvertised opportunities.

If your agent hasn't been participating in prior project meetings, make sure he or she gets brought up to speed by informing them of your office space requirements. It will now be up to the agent to provide you with a report of available alternatives, which come reasonably close to the type of space you have defined.

Keep in mind, if you have determined that your ideal space should be 5,000 square feet, it is reasonable for the agent to return a list of properties between 4,000 and 6,000 square feet.

Depending on whether a space is configured efficiently, it is possible that a slightly smaller or larger space will make more sense. Having a square footage range will also give you more options from which to choose.

Property Analysis

With the help of you real estate agent, if using, develop a list of office space vacancies that fit your leasing requirements.

Include as much detail as possible for each property, such as cost per square foot, size of space, availability of parking and other amenities. See the example below.

PROPERTY ANALYSIS EXAMPLE									
Location	Area/ Square Feet	Lease Term	Rental Rate/ Square Feet	Additional Expenses	Estimate of Additional Expenses**	Rental Rate w/ Expenses	Annual Cost of Occupancy	Growth Potential	Comments
800 W. State St.	5,742	5 Years	$25.50	Janitorial	$1.75	$27.25	$156,470	Additional 2,500 square feet available	Parking is tight
715 S. Capital Blvd.	6,029	3 Years	$27.85	None All expenses are included	$0	$27.85	$167,908	Additional 4,000 square feet available	Good Parking, but difficult access
2037 Technology Dr.	6,197	5 years	$29.25	None All expenses are included	$0	$29.25	$181,262	None	On-site cafeteria, good parking and access
300 E. 41st St.	6,422	5 Years	$24.95	Utilities Janitorial	$3.00	$27.95	$179,495	None	Older building, no free parking, additional storage space available at reduced cost.

Once you have created a list of available spaces, review the options to determine which properties you wish to tour. If any of the alternatives presented are obviously undesirable, cross them off the list; then make arrangements to tour the rest.

After visiting each of the spaces that remain on the list, determine the two or three properties that best meet your requirement. These should all be properties that you would be willing to operate your business from.

5 | Space Planning

When you have determined your top two or three choices, it is important to have a preliminary space plan drawn for each property to see how they can be configured to best suit your needs.

How your business will fit in a particular space and what changes will be required is important because a landlord's economic terms will be dependent on the extent of construction and upgrades that your business will require.

Preliminary Space Planning

An architect should create a preliminary space plan for each of the proposed spaces. These initial space plans are called a "test-fit." This is a critical step in determining how many square feet will be required to accommodate your needs in each building and which spaces will offer the most efficient layout. Certain office space programs will lay out better in some buildings than others, making the test-fit process an important step in comparing alternatives.

Although several buildings may have spaces that appear to be similarly suitable for your business, once the test-fits are completed, the differences in function and efficiency may be significant.

Cost of Space Planning

The expense of preliminary space planning is typically paid for by the landlord; it is part of his or her cost of doing business. Landlords either employ in-house designers, or they outsource their space planning needs. You can also bring in your own architect to design the preliminary plan, if you prefer.

If your requirement is fairly simple, in order to save time, it may make sense to sketch in your changes on a copy of the floorplan. You may also be able to negotiate a slightly more favorable rental rate if you don't engage the services of the landlord's space planner.

On the other hand, if your requirement is complex, it will be necessary to meet with a space planner and have them draw up a space plan from scratch. Make sure you are aware of what the building owner's standard finish includes. If you desire more luxurious offices, consider upgrading carpeting and lighting.

Tenant Improvement Allowance

Part of the space planning process is determining what changes, if any, will be required and which party will pay for the cost. Changes or enhancements to a particular space are considered tenant improvements and may be covered under a tenant improvement allowance offered by the landlord. A tenant improvement allowance is usually a specific dollar amount that allows for certain changes, such as having the carpet replaced, having the interior painted, and/or having walls constructed or demolished.

If the space is in shell condition, the tenant improvement amount may allow for most, if not all, of the build-out of the space. There are also instances when a space is offered without a tenant improvement allowance. In this case the landlord intends for any desired changes or improvements to be at the tenant's expense.

If you happen to be able to take a space in "as-is" condition, be sure to inquire whether there will be a discount in the rental rate. It could be that you can save $1.00 per square foot or more because you have no need for a built-in construction or tenant improvement allowance.

Working With a Space Planner

When you begin meeting with a space planner to design office space, consider all the factors that would make the space ideal for your business. Although volumes of information have been published concerning the design of workspaces, the best advice you can follow is to consult an expert, a professional space designer/planner.

Keep in mind, the quantity and level of space improvements will have a direct bearing on the rental rate. The cost of improvements, over and above the tenant improvement allowance, will be paid for by the tenant.

The space planner's role is to help you create an environment that fits your needs today and that can be adapted to your future requirements. Your final floorplan should insure that work areas help employees to accomplish job functions comfortably and efficiently, that workflow patterns are productive, and that the end solution meets management objectives.

Generally, the space planner will draw up a preliminary plan, using the building's standard finishes. Your designer can assist you in choosing alternative or upgraded finishes, if you are willing to pay the difference, and have a desire that your space has a different look and feel from the rest of the building.

Once you have chosen a particular space and are moving toward lease negotiation, the preliminary space plan will be the basis for final construction drawings.

The preliminary plan will be used in conjunction with other factors to determine the rental rate during the proposal process. Remember that the cost of building out office space is not free, it is included in your rental rate and amortized over the life of the lease. If you vacate the space before lease end, you will usually be held responsible for any unamortized construction and improvement expenses.

6 | Developing your Request for Proposal (RFP)

Once you have narrowed your search to two or three buildings and completed preliminary space planning, you should prepare a Request for Proposal (RFP) for each location. The RFP process creates competition among landlords for your business.

A written request for proposal should be submitted to the building owner (or his or her agent) for each of the buildings on your final list of alternatives.

Before sending out the RFP's, make sure any option you may be considering is noted. Your negotiation leverage will be greatly reduced if you leave out a provision that is important to you. For example, if you would like an option to expand, ask for the building owner's position on expansion in the RFP.

Preparing an RFP

In order to make a fair comparison of your short-listed alternatives, the information contained in each RFP needs to be consistent. An effective RFP should be customized to your specific needs. Remove items that are not applicable to your business and/or add items that may be unique to your specific office requirements.

Your RFP should include the following:

Tenant Information
State your company's complete name including information on the corporate entity.

Building Address
Include the precise address of the building and suite number you are interested in leasing. It is important that the address is stated accurately to insure there are no misunderstandings about the exact location of the space you desire. If available, include a copy of the floorplan as an attachment to the RFP.

Square Footage of Office Suite (Area)
The amount of square footage you require. If the space has already been configured into individual office suites, state the amount of square footage available in the subject suite.

Load Factor

Request the load factor for the building. The load factor refers to the portion of the building's common areas attributed to your suite. To compare different office spaces, you have to know the exact usable square footage of each space you are considering. For more information see Office Space Load Factor on page 8.

Lease Term
State your preferred lease term. Landlords are typically willing to make more concessions for longer-term leases.

For tenants, however, a long-term lease has both benefits and risks. The benefit is knowing that the premises are available at a predictable cost for the long term. The risk is that your company's space needs may change and you may be locked into paying above-market rent if demand for office space subsequently declines.

Building owners are motivated to enter into long-term leases (5 years or more) to protect their cash flow and minimize the risk of having vacant space. In most situations, longer term leases will be less expensive than their shorter term counterparts.

Also, if there are tenant improvement costs to be amortized over the life of the lease, longer-term leases will be less expensive on a monthly basis. (This is simple math: let's assume $10,000 in tenant improvements, financed at 10%. A three-year lease would cost an additional $306 per month and a five-year lease would cost an additional $183 per month.)

It is also important that you take your growth potential into consideration. It would not be smart to sign a 1,200 square foot, five-year lease when you anticipate your company will grow and that will need 2,500 square feet in three years.

Lease Commencement Date

The date you wish to begin the lease. When choosing a commencement date, if possible consider timing it to a non-peak month for your business. An accounting business, for instance, that has a high volume in the months leading up to April 15th should plan their commencement date for some time after the tax season. This ensures they won't be in the middle of a move during a busy time.

If circumstances require a less desirable commencement date, consider altering your lease expiration date to a more convenient time of the year by varying the lease term by a month or two in either direction. For example, if the accounting firm mentioned above was considering entering into a 60-month lease commencing on March 1st, it would be appropriate for this business to request a 66-month term, giving them an expiration date five and a half years later on August 31st. Under this scenario, there will be an opportunity to renegotiate or relocate at the end of the lease term at a more convenient time of year.

Occupancy Date

Usually the occupancy date is the same as the commencement date; however, tenants are sometimes allowed to take possession of the space before the commencement date in order to move in and set up furnishings and equipment for their needs. Depending on the market for office space in your area, it doesn't hurt to ask for an occupancy date at least two weeks prior to the lease commencement date.

If the real estate market is in a downturn, consider asking for an occupancy date of two to three months prior to the lease commencement date. In essence, the difference between the occupancy date and the commencement date is considered free rent.

Rental Rate

Ask for the rental rate and detailed information on any additional expenses your business will be responsible for.

You will also want a clarification of what is included in the rent rate. See page 5 for detailed information on rental rate structures and types of leases.

For instance, while many buildings offer Full Service leases, which are all inclusive, some buildings do not include janitorial service, or require the tenants pay their own utilities. If the base rental rate is low, but you are required to pay for several additional expenses, you may not be getting as good a deal as it seems.

Security Deposit

Request information on the amount and timing of the security deposit. A typical security deposit is equivalent to one or two months of rent and is paid when the lease is signed.

Whether or not you will have to pay a security deposit will be based on office market conditions and your company's creditworthiness. Companies deemed to have less than sterling credit will almost certainly be required to pay a deposit. Typically, a security deposit is equal to one or two month's rent and will be returned to your company at the end of the lease, assuming minimal wear and tear on the space.

Operating Expenses

In leases that include building operating expenses, a portion of the rent will go toward real estate taxes, property insurance and common area maintenance.

Because the cost of these items fluctuate and tend to go up from year to year, most building owner's require tenant's to participate in the annual escalations of these expenses.

Ideally, you want the building owner to agree that no additional expenses will be charged during the first year of the lease. This is referred to as a Base Year Allowance. Under a base year allowance, the portion of your rental rate attributed to building operating expenses is equal to the actual expenses during the first year of your lease.

Expansion Option

If your business is dynamic in nature, request an expansion option to allow for future growth. There are two options that allow for expansion, a Right of First Offer, and a Right of First Refusal. A Right of First Offer obligates your landlord to present any space that becomes available in the building to you first before marketing it to third parties.

A Right of First Refusal obligates the landlord to bring you any deals he or she is willing to sign with third parties for space in the building and allow you to match the deal and preempt the third party. A Right of First Refusal is a much more powerful option, as it gives you more time to make a decision. You won't have to enter into an obligation for the space until another party is prepared to sign a lease.

Your ability to negotiate an expansion option and an option to renew will depend on market conditions and will be subject to any commitments that have been made to current building tenants. When market conditions favor tenants, options are easier to get; when conditions swing to the landlord's favor, they are more difficult.

Lease Extension Option (Renewal Clause)

Request an option to renew or a lease extension. An option to renew confirms that you will be able to renew the lease at the end of your initial lease term. Whether you plan on staying in the space or not, it is important to have this option. This particular clause does not obligate you to renew the space; it is simply an option that helps you maintain flexibility.

When negotiating a lease extension, the ideal arrangement for a tenant is to attempt to maintain the current lease rate with a percentage increase to account for inflation. Most building owners, however, will require that the extension be negotiated at the market rate for space in the building at the end of the initial lease term.

Space Planning

If desired, request that the building owner provide a professional space planner to assist in designing the space to your specifications. (Further aspects of the space planning process are described in Chapter 5.)

Tenant Improvement Allowance

Ask for the tenant improvement allowance of the subject space. If a preliminary space plan has been drawn, include it as an attachment to determine if the proposed allowance will be sufficient to cover the changes.

Assignment and Sublease Clause

The assignment and sublease clause is a very important part of the lease document. As such, you should request, up front, for it to be included in any lease you enter in to.

Ask for the right to assign or sublease the leased premises at any time during the lease, with landlord's consent, which shall not be unreasonably withheld or delayed.

Access

Let the building owner know what type of access your employees will need to the building. State what your typical office hours are and if you will need after hours and weekend access.

Mechanical Systems

Request information on the building's Heating, Ventilation and Air Conditioning (HVAC) system. Many buildings have an energy-management system in place that will automatically cut back heating and cooling after business hours and on weekends. If you have a 24-hour business or often work after-hours, you may require additional heat or air conditioning. Some landlords charge by the hour for this service; ask if there is a cost for after-hours HVAC usage.

Fire/Safety Systems

Request a description of the fire and safety systems in the building.

Building Security

Request information on building security and state any specifics required to meet your needs. If you are planning on installing your own security system within the suite, check to see if there will be any limitations placed on the type or scope of your proposed system.

Elevators

Enquire as to how many and what type of elevator service (passenger or freight) is available in the building, if applicable.

Parking

Request information on the number of available parking spaces and if there are any costs associated with parking. State the specific requirement for the number of spaces needed to provide adequate parking for your employees and visitors.

Public Transportation

Request details on public transportation in the vicinity of the building.

Additional Storage Space

If you have additional storage needs, check to see if the building leases basement or other under-utilized space at a lower rate for archive file storage, etc.

Building Ownership

Request information on the ownership of the building.

Property Management

Request that the landlord provide information on who manages the property, including the company name and whether there are property management employees on site. A good property management team can make the difference between a well-run building and one that has maintenance issues.

Building Amenities

Ask for information on any amenities that are in or near the building.

Standard Lease

Request a copy of the landlord's standard lease. While the standard lease document is subject to revision throughout the negotiation process, it is another tool to help you familiarize yourself with the terms and conditions of leasing space in a particular building.

Submittal Information

Include submittal instructions and a deadline for responses. The RFP responses should be directed to your commercial real estate agent, if using. Any questions about the RFP or requests for additional information should also be directed to your agent.

Example Request for Proposal

Tenant Information:	The Easton Group, a Washington Corporation
Premises:	Presidio Center 3180 Creekside Dr., Suite 210
Area:	6,827 square feet
Load Factor:	Is there a load factor in this building? If so, please describe and state both the rentable and usable square footage of the proposed space.
Lease Commencement Date:	April 1
Occupancy Date:	March 15, tenant requests access to the space two weeks prior to the lease commencement date to set up furnishings and equipment.
Lease Term:	Five (5) years
Rental Rate:	Propose the most aggressive rental rate possible. State any rent escalations during the lease term and any additional operating expenses that are not included in the rental rate.
Security Deposit:	Is a security deposit required for the space? If so, state the amount and terms of the deposit.

Operating Expenses:	Define what services are included in the rental rate, and what additional operating expenses will be paid by the tenant. For expenses that are included within the rental rate, Tenant requests an allowance equal to the actual cost of the first full calendar year of the lease (Base Year). Provide a history of actual building operating expenses during the last three calendar years.
Tenant Improvement Allowance:	What is the tenant improvement allowance for improvements to the proposed suite?
Option to Renew:	Tenant requests one (1) option to renew the lease upon expiration, upon the same terms and conditions as the original lease, with the exception of rent, which will be at the market rate for space in the building, to be agreed upon by both tenant and landlord. Tenant will give landlord 120 days written notice of the tenant's intent to renew this lease.
Expansion Option:	Describe how any potential need for expansion space can be met in this building. Tenant requests a Right of First Refusal on any adjoining space to Suite 210 that becomes available during the lease term.
Space Planning:	Tenant will require a space planner to prepare a plan, at the landlord's expense, to determine if the proposed suite can meet its office space requirements.
Assignment & Sublease:	Tenant will require the right to assign or sublease the leased premises at any time during the lease term, with Landlord's consent, which shall not be unreasonably withheld or delayed.
Signage:	What tenant signage will be provided at the landlord's expense? Are there additional signage opportunities available at the tenant's expense?
Access:	Tenant requires 24-hour access to the leased premises.

Mechanical Systems:	Describe the building's heating, ventilation and cooling (HVAC) system, including square feet per zone, hours of service, and whether there is a charge for after-hours usage.
Fire/Safety Systems:	Describe the building's fire protection and safety systems.
Building Security:	Does the landlord provide security in and around the building? What restrictions, if any, does the landlord have on tenants installing their own security system on the leased premises?
Elevators:	How many elevators does the building have? Include information on both freight and passenger elevators.
Parking:	Provide information on the parking ratio for the building and how it will accommodate the tenant's requirement for forty-two parking spaces (37 employee and 5 visitor spaces). Describe any additional costs associated with parking.
Public Transportation:	Provide detail on availability of public transportation in the vicinity of the building.
Additional Storage Space:	Does the building have any additional storage space available at a discounted rental rate?
Building Ownership:	Give an overview of the building ownership.
Property Management:	What property management company is responsible for maintaining the building and are they located on site?
Standard Lease:	Please include a copy of your standard lease for the proposed building.

Building Amenities: Describe amenities available to tenants of the building.

Submittal Information: Pease submit your response within 10 business days.

Distributing the RFP's

Distribute the completed RFP's to the appropriate building owners, or building owner representatives. Keep a record of when each request was sent, and expect to hear a reply within one to two weeks. It is also a good idea to follow up with a phone call after the requests have been sent. Check to make sure the information was received, and whether there are any questions.

If you have not heard back from a specific building owner within two weeks, give them a call to find out if there is a reason for the delay. It may be that the space you are interested in has already been leased, and the building owner has no reason to respond to your request for proposal. (A conscientious building owner should notify you if this is the case, however, that doesn't always happen.)

7 | Evaluating the Proposals

Once the RFP responses have been collected, compare and analyze each of the alternatives.

It is essential that you have more than one proposal to compare. If, for some reason, you only receive one proposal, it will be necessary to go back and request a proposal from the next possible candidate on your list.

One method of cataloging and evaluating the proposals is to prepare a Proposal Evaluation for each RFP response. The first two columns of the Proposal Evaluation show what information you requested. The remaining columns show the response to each item from the landlord and whether or not this result is acceptable to your company.

You should also take the time to contact a random mix of the tenants in each building and assess their level of satisfaction with the landlord and management. Instead of asking the landlord for references, compile a list of tenants in each of the prospective buildings. Call three or four companies of various sizes in each building in order to get a fair appraisal. A summary of these comments should also be included on the Proposal Evaluation form.

Proposal Evaluation

Proposal Items	Tenant's Request	Landlord's Response	Decision
Premises	3180 Creekside Drive, Suite 210		
Area/Sq. Ft.	6,827 square feet	6,827 square feet	Acceptable
Load Factor	Load factor percentage	18%	Acceptable
Lease Commencement Date	April 1	April 1	Acceptable
Occupancy Date	March 15	March 15	Acceptable
Lease Term	Five (5) years.	Five (5) years.	Acceptable
Rental Rate	Most aggressive rental rate.	$29.75/sq. ft.	Negotiating
Rent Escalation	Amount of escalation, if any.	$0.50/sq. ft., annually	Acceptable
Security Deposit	Define security deposit.	Equal to one month's rent.	Acceptable
Operating Expenses	Requested a Base Year lease.	Base Year lease.	Acceptable
Tenant Improvements	Amount of tenant improvement allowance.	$15.00 per square foot.	Negotiating
Option to Renew	One (1) renewal option with 120 days' notice.	One (1) renewal option with 180 days' notice.	Acceptable
Expansion Option	Describe expansion availability.	Only if tenant on either side relocates.	Acceptable
Space Planning	Landlord to pay for the cost of a space planner or architect.	Space planner to be provided by landlord.	Acceptable
Assignment & Subleasing	Tenant to have the ability to assign or sublease the premises.	Lease to include assignment and subleasing clause.	Acceptable
Signage	Landlord provides signs identifying Tenant in lobby and at the Tenant's suite entry at landlord's expense.	Landlord provides signs identifying Tenant in lobby and at the Tenant's suite entry at landlord's expense.	Acceptable
Access	24-hour access.	24-hour access card reader at doors.	Acceptable
Mechanical Systems	Describe the HVAC system.	Service runs from 7 a.m. to 7 p.m. M -F, overtime charges are $50/hour.	Unacceptable, negotiating better rate.
Fire/Safety Systems	Describe fire and safety protection.	Building is has sprinklers per code, emergency exit signage and fire alarms throughout.	Acceptable

Proposal Items	Tenant's Request	Landlord's Response	Decision
Building Security	What security is provided?	24-hour monitoring by security company.	Acceptable
Elevators	Describe elevators.	2 passenger, 1 freight	Acceptable
Parking	Describe available parking. Is there a charge for parking?	Four parking spaces per 1,000 square feet of leased space. No charge for parking.	Acceptable
Public Transportation	Availability of public transportation.	Building is located adjacent to a public transit stop.	Acceptable
Additional Storage Space	Is additional storage space available?	Yes, at $12.00 per square foot.	Acceptable
Building Owner-ship	Describe building's ownership	Owner name and address has been provided.	Acceptable
Property Management	Outline the property management of the building.	Property management is provided by Commercial Properties, they have a maintenance supervisor located on-site.	Acceptable
Building Amenities	Include available amenities.	Coffee shop in lobby, mail and overnight drop boxes.	Acceptable
Standard Lease	Requested a copy of standard lease.	Standard lease was included with proposal.	Reviewing
References	Called 4 tenants in the building. All were satisfied or very satisfied with the building's management.	N/A	Acceptable

Follow up on any incomplete items or questions and continue negotiating on any terms that are unacceptable. Your goal is to achieve terms that work for your business, or a reasonable compromise, for each property.

Once any remaining questions have been answered and terms are generally acceptable it is time to choose which property best suits the needs of your business. Consolidating RFP responses for each building in a Proposal Summary, example below, will show you at a glance how the various options stack up.

Proposal Summary

Proposal Items	Proposal 1	Proposal 2	Proposal 3
Premises	3180 Creekside Dr.	8435 Perimeter Way	8202 La Vista Pkwy.
Area/Sq. Ft.	6,827 square feet	6,322 square feet	5,877 square feet
Load Factor	18%	19%	16%
Lease Commence-ment Date	April 1	April 15	May 1
Occupancy Date	March 15	April 1	May 1
Lease Term	Five (5) years.	Five (5) years.	Five (5) years.
Rental Rate	$29.75/sq. ft.	$27.25/sq. ft.	$32.50/sq. ft.
Rent Escalation	$0.50/sq. ft. annually	3% annually	3.5% annually
Security Deposit	One month's rent	1st & last month's rent	One month's rent
Operating Expenses	Base Year	Base Year	Base Year
Tenant Improvements	$15.00 per square foot	$13.00 per square foot	$17.00 per square foot
Option to Renew	One (1) renewal option.	One (1) renewal option.	One (1) renewal option.
Expansion Option	Right of First Offer	Right of First Offer	Right of First Refusal
Space Planning	Landlord provided	Landlord provided	Landlord provided
Assignment & Subleasing	Included in lease	Included in lease	Included in lease
Signage	Landlord will provide door and lobby sign.	Monument sign available at tenant's expense.	Landlord will provide door and lobby sign.
Access	Landlord to provide 24-hour access card reader at main door.	24-hour access is available.	24-hour access is available.
Mechanical Systems	Service runs from 7 a.m. to 7 p.m. M - F, overtime charges are $50/hour.	No energy management system. Thermostat can be overridden at any time.	Service runs from 6 a.m. to 8 p.m. M - F, overtime charges are $38/hour.
Fire/Safety Systems	Building has sprinklers, lighted emergency exits. Fire alarms throughout building.	Building has sprinklers, lighted emergency exits. Fire alarms throughout building.	Building has sprinklers, lighted emergency exits. Fire alarms throughout building.

Proposal Items	Proposal 1	Proposal 2	Proposal 3
Building Security	24-hour security monitoring provided by security company.	24-hour security monitoring provided by security company.	Security guard in lobby. 24-hour parking lot monitoring.
Elevators	2 passenger, 1 freight	1 passenger, 1 freight	4 passenger, 1 freight
Parking	4 parking spaces per 1000 square feet. No assigned parking.	3.5 parking spaces per 1000 square feet. No assigned parking.	Parking garage attached to building. No free parking.
Public Transportation	Adjacent to transit stop	None	2 blocks from bus stop.
Additional Storage Space	Yes, at $12.00 per square foot.	Not available.	Not available.
Building Ownership	Owner name and address has been provided.	Owner name and address has been provided.	Owner name and address has been provided.
Property Management	Commercial Properties, maintenance supervisor on-site.	Horizon Management. No employees on site.	Premier Properties, on-site management office.
Building Amenities	Coffee shop in lobby, mail and overnight drop boxes.	Mail and overnight drop boxes.	Cafeteria, shopping in lower level.
Standard Lease	Standard lease was included with proposal.	Standard lease was included with proposal.	Standard lease was included with proposal.
References	Called 4 tenants in the building. All were satisfied to very satisfied with the building's management.	Called 3 tenants in the building. There have been problems with the responsiveness of the management company.	Called 4 tenants in the building. Three were happy with the way the building is managed, one was unhappy.

When you have determined which building seems to make the most sense for your business, go back over the proposal and make sure that the terms are acceptable to you. Most major lease negotiation items will be founded on the proposal, so if there is a term you would like changed or improved upon, now is the time to ask.

An analysis of the proposal summary will assist you in making your final facility choice.

8 | Letter of Intent

With a decision made on the best choice of space for your business, prepare and submit a Letter of Intent (LOI) to the landlord of the selected space. An LOI is essentially an offer to lease space and outlines the terms under which your company is willing to enter into a lease agreement. Typically, the LOI will be non-binding and there will be no commitment by either party until a lease agreement is fully executed.

In most cases, it is best to focus on a single property during the LOI phase. However, when market conditions favor landlords and you are at risk of not getting your first-choice property, it is acceptable to submit two or more LOI's simultaneously. To adhere to leasing etiquette it is recommended that you inform the landlords or their agents when multiple LOI's are being submitted.

Negotiating the Letter of Intent

Use the terms from the final RFP response as the basis for your Letter of Intent, but don't be afraid to push again in certain areas, particularly on the rent. Landlords expect several rounds of back-and-forth during this stage of the leasing process and will likely respond to your Letter of Intent with a counter-offer. Offering five to ten percent less than the proposed rent from the RFP will give you the opportunity to find out if the landlord has any additional room for negotiation.

Once the terms of the Letter of Intent are fully agreed upon by all parties to the agreement, it should be signed by both tenant and landlord. A fully executed Letter of Intent signifies readiness to move forward with a lease.

Example Letter of Intent

This Letter of Intent is entered into for the purpose of stating the intent of all parties regarding space available for lease at 3180 Creekside Drive, Suite 210. Subject to the execution of a mutually acceptable Lease Agreement, this Letter of Intent will establish the basic terms and conditions for the Lease Agreement.

Landlord: Rainier Properties

Tenant: The Easton Group

Location/Address: 3180 Creekside Dr., Suite 210

Use: General Office

Approximate Size: 6,827

Lease Commencement Date: April 1

Occupancy Date: March 15

Lease Term: Five (5) years

Rental Rate: $29.50 per square foot

Rent Escalation: $0.50 per square foot annually, beginning in second year of lease term.

Security Deposit: One (1) month's rent

Tenant Improvements: $15.00 per square foot allowance

Option to Renew: Tenant shall have the right to renew its lease for five (5) years with 180 days' notice given prior to lease expiration date. The terms and conditions for the renewal period shall be the same as those for the initial lease term except the rent shall be adjusted to Fair Market Value for comparable space.

Expansion Option: Tenant shall have a Right of First Offer on any adjacent space.

Signage: Landlord shall provide tenant with signage on lobby directory and a plaque at tenant's entrance.

The terms and conditions referenced above shall not be binding upon Landlord or Tenant until such time as the Lease and any related documents have been reviewed and approved by Tenant and Tenant's legal counsel and such Lease and documents have been fully executed by Landlord and Tenant.

Landlord: _____

Tenant: _____

With the lease terms agreed upon and a fully executed Letter of Intent, the landlord will prepare a lease specific to the space you intend to occupy, complete with your company information and the negotiated terms.

9 | Negotiating the Best Possible Lease Terms

As previously mentioned, office space is among the highest expenses a business incurs, second only to employee wages. In order to obtain competitive lease terms, a tenant should understand not only his or her own rights and the leverage he or she brings into the lease, but also the compatibility of their goals with the landlord's. An attorney experienced in commercial leases will be invaluable in assisting tenants in:

- Determining the rights of the parties.

- Understanding the significance of all lease terms.

- Recognizing the leverage and goals of landlord and tenant.

- Evaluating the costs of a lease, including any hidden costs.

- Negotiating all the terms of a lease.

The tenant who knows not only what he or she wants, but also what the landlord is looking for, will emerge from negotiation with a more favorable lease than the tenant who only considers his or her own goals without regard to the goals of the landlord.

Lease Review

In general, no two office leases are alike; some are very lengthy and complex while others are short and fairly simple. Regardless of the size of the document it is imperative that you fully understand each part of the lease agreement. It is also recommended that you have the lease reviewed by an attorney that specializes in commercial lease agreements. While you may have already reviewed the standard lease document during the proposal process, keep in mind, a number of clauses may have been added or changed during negotiations.

Reviewing the lease for business terms is a matter of matching up the negotiated proposal terms with what appears in the lease document. Your attorney should review the legal language of the lease. The building owner or landlord will expect you and your attorney to make changes to this document; this is part of the negotiation process.

In addition to the business terms, office leases include a variety of clauses that benefit the building owner at your expense. Your attorney should spot these red flags and work to negotiate a lease agreement that is fair to both parties.

Some of the most common of these potentially biased provisions include:

- Requiring the tenant to pay any tax increases as a result of the landlord selling the building.

- Allowing the landlord to terminate the lease for his or her convenience.

- Imposing severe restrictions on a tenant's ability to sub-lease the space.

Your ability to negotiate changes in these provisions is dependent on how much leverage you have. Are other companies vying for the space? Has the space been vacant for a long time? You may be able to negotiate more favorable terms on the following key points.

Grace Period and Notice

It is important to ensure you receive a reasonable grace period and adequate notice before the landlord has a right to charge either a late fee or penalty for delinquent payments. This is necessary because many default clauses allow the landlord to accelerate the balance of the rent payments due under the lease if the tenant is in default.

If the grace period and notice provision seem unduly harsh, ask for more time.

Rent Escalation

Fixed rent over longer-term leases is relatively rare, more likely, the lease will have a rent escalation provision. With a lease escalation provision the rental rate will typically be increased in one of two ways – based on the Consumer Price Index (CPI) or with a fixed dollar amount.

If your lease calls for rent escalations to be tied to the CPI, request a CPI rent increase that does not kick in for at least two years. Then, ask for a cap on the amount of each year's increase. The benefit of having your rent escalation tied to the CPI is that it is relatively fair. However, in times of inflation, without a cap, you could see your rent increase significantly.

The other option for a rent escalation clause is a fixed increase in the form of a dollar amount or percentage, such as a $500 annual increase in rent each year of the lease term. For instance, if the rent is $2,000 the first year, the rent would increase to $2,500 the second year and $3,000 the third year. A fixed amount will be simple to budget for and there won't be any surprises.

Operating Expenses and Tax Escalations

Most office leases require the tenant to pay increases in building operating expenses and taxes. Typically, rent adjustments do not become effective until the first anniversary of the lease.

You should ensure that the base amounts for taxes and operating expenses are for a fully assessed and operational building. If not, these expenses may jump when the building is finally assessed for taxes and is fully occupied, as additional tenants place extra demands on the building's systems and services.

Only those costs that are directly related to the building's operation and benefit all tenants should be included in the operating expenses that are passed through to a tenant. The following fees are not considered building operating expenses and should not be included in these charges:

- Marketing or advertising of the building.

- Any expense incurred by the owner for a particular tenant or lease.

- Capital improvements to the building.

When analyzing the cost of office space, take into account any additional expenses that the landlord may pass on to you. Some leases require the tenant pay for janitorial services, building security, electricity, HVAC (heating, ventilating and air conditioning), maintenance and repairs. If the landlord is charging you separately for these services, try to negotiate a fixed fee or a cap on the amount.

If the rate quoted is full service, and the building owner will be charging extra for HVAC services supplied after-hours or on weekends, you should also negotiate a fixed fee or cap on these expenses, as well.

Tenant Improvements

As discussed previously, you may have been able to negotiate a contribution by the landlord for improving the premises.

Detailed plans and specifications for the work to be performed should be attached to the lease as an exhibit. Obligations of the building owner and tenant with respect to the payment for and construction of the improvements needs to be spelled out.

Additionally, most leases provide that the tenant cannot make any alterations or improvements without the landlord's consent. Ask for a clause that says you can make alterations or improvements with the landlord's consent, and that the consent shall not be unreasonably withheld or delayed.

The key here is the phrase "not to be unreasonably withheld or delayed". Without this addition a landlord can stonewall the process by taking an undue amount of time to review your request.

Repairs and Replacements

Be aware of a clause that says that at the end of the lease you have to return the premises in their original condition. With the advice of your attorney, try to negotiate a clause that states the following, or something similar: "The premises will be returned to the Landlord at the end of the tenancy in the same condition as at the beginning of the tenancy, excluding (1) ordinary wear and tear, (2) damage by fire and unavoidable casualty not the fault of the Tenant and (3) alterations previously approved by the Landlord."

This language will offer you much more protection in the event that the premises have changed since the inception of your lease agreement.

Assignment and Subleasing

In the absence of a provision to the contrary, a tenant is free to assign or sublet a lease. Most landlords, however, insist on a clause to the effect that a tenant must obtain the landlord's approval before an assignment or subletting is permitted.

This is also an area where the phrase "and that the consent shall not be unreasonably withheld or delayed" should be added after "…is prohibited without landlord's consent."

Generally, courts have determined that a landlord cannot reasonably withhold consent if the proposed assignee or sublessee:

- Is a financially responsible party.

- Is a suitable tenant for the building and space.

- Has an identity or business character that conforms to the standards of the property.

- Uses the premises in a legal fashion.

- Is in accordance with applicable laws and zoning requirements, and has all necessary permits to perform business.

- Will require only minimal alterations to the premises.

It should be noted that a lessee's right to assign or sublease is meaningless if the use clause in the lease is so restrictive that it would be difficult to find another tenant with a conforming use. Therefore, you should attempt to make the use clause as general as possible. Request that the use clause be drafted to include "any lawful purposes."

Start-up companies, in particular, should negotiate enough flexibility in the assignment and subleasing clause to allow for mergers, reorganizations and share ownership changes.

Watch out for a clause that says a change in more than 50 percent of the company's stock ownership will be deemed an assignment that is prohibited without the landlord's approval. As the company grows and new people invest in the company, this clause can be inadvertently triggered.

Maintenance and Repair

You should be guided by the principle that if the lease does not place obligation on the landlord, your company, as the tenant, is responsible. Accordingly, who is responsible for what repair obligations should be detailed in the lease.

Also attempt to include in the lease remedies against the landlord in the event that the landlord fails to perform the required repairs. The remedy can take the form of a clause permitting the tenant to make the repairs and to deduct the cost of such repairs from rent if the landlord fails to make the repairs within a certain period of time.

Default and Remedies

Many leases contain harsh default and eviction terms. Therefore, it is important to insure that your landlord cannot terminate the lease unless your company fails to comply with a contractual provision, receives adequate notice of such failure and does not cure the problem in a timely fashion.

A distinction should be made between monetary and non-monetary defaults, and the time periods given to cure the problem should be reflected accordingly.   .

Renewal and Expansion Options

Renewal and expansion options give you additional breathing room in both time and space over the original lease term. As a result, try to obtain as many renewal and expansion options as possible. Even if the option terms do not appear to be particularly generous, they can only be beneficial, because your company can always choose not to exercise an option.

Final Lease Review

The lease document checklist below will assist you in reviewing the lease. As leases vary from landlord to landlord, this checklist is not intended to cover every possible aspect or substitute for review by an attorney; however, it will allow you to make a more thorough and knowledgeable review of your lease agreement.

Lease Document Checklist

Parties to the Agreement

☐ Is your company's name represented correctly?

☐ Has your business entity been stated, e.g., corporation, LLC?

Space Characteristics

☐ Confirm the address of the building and suite number, if applicable, are accurate.

☐ Verify the square footage of the space is stated correctly.

☐ What is the rentable square footage?

☐ What is the usable square footage?

Permitted Uses of the Premises

☐ What uses of the premises are permitted?

☐ Is the permitted use clause broad enough for possible changes in the business?

☐ Is the permitted use clause broad enough for potential assignments or subleases?

☐ Can the use clause be drafted to include "any lawful purposes"?

☐ Can uses be changed with landlord's consent, which consent cannot be unreasonably withheld or delayed?

Primary Lease Term

☐ What is the commencement date of the lease?

☐ What happens if the space is not ready on the commencement date? Is there rent abatement, monetary damages, right to cancel the lease, or other remedies specified?

☐ What is the termination date?

☐ Does the landlord have the right to terminate early without cause?

☐ Does the tenant have the right to terminate early by payment of a fee?

Security deposit

☐ Is a security deposit required?

☐ If so, is the amount stated correctly?

☐ Will interest be paid on the security deposit?

☐ Does the lease provide for the return of the tenant's security deposit within a set number of days after termination of the lease?

Base Rental Rate

☐ Is the base rental rate for the term of the lease reflected accurately?

☐ Are there rent escalations?

☐ Is there a cap on any rent increases?

Late Charges

☐ Is there a reasonable grace period before a late charge is assessed?

☐ Is the late charge reasonable?

Operating Expenses

☐ What is defined as a building operating expense?

☐ When does the landlord expect payment for operating expenses?

☐ What documentation is the landlord required to provide to the tenant showing the actual expenses for the building?

Real Estate Taxes

☐ Does the tenant have to pay a portion of the real estate taxes?

☐ Does the tenant have to pay increased taxes that may occur on sale of the building?

Tenant Improvements

☐ What tenant improvements will be necessary?

☐ What is the cost of the tenant improvements?

☐ How much time will it take to complete the tenant improvements?

☐ Will the landlord contribute to the cost of the tenant improvements?

☐ What approvals will be necessary?

☐ What permits will be necessary?

☐ Is it clear which improvements will be paid for by the landlord and which will be paid for by the tenant?

☐ Upon lease termination does the landlord or the tenant own the improvements?

HVAC and Mechanical Systems

☐ Are there provisions made for after-hours, weekend and holiday service? What are the charges?

☐ Does the tenant have a remedy for service interruption?

Repairs and Replacements

☐ What responsibility does the tenant have for repairs or replacements?

☐ What responsibility does the landlord have for repairs or replacements?

☐ At the end of the tenancy, is tenant obligated to return the premises in same condition as at the beginning of tenancy, excluding (1) ordinary wear and tear, (2) damage by fire and other unavoidable casualty, and (3) alterations previously approved by landlord?

Utilities

☐ Is the landlord or the tenant responsible for the cost of utilities?

☐ If the landlord is responsible for utilities, what are the standard hours of operation for the heating and cooling system?

Assignment and Subleasing

☐ Is the landlord's written approval required?

☐ Does the lease state the landlord's approval shall not be unreasonably withheld or delayed?

☐ What standard is there for approval? Does the landlord have absolute discretion, or is he or she bound by a reasonable approval process?

☐ If the assignment or sublease is at a higher price than the base rent, who keeps the excess, or is there a split between landlord and tenant?

☐ Can the lease be assigned to affiliates of the tenant without landlord approval?

Destruction

☐ Is there a right of cancellation for the tenant in the event of destruction?

☐ What obligation does the landlord have to rebuild the premises?

☐ Does the tenant share in any proceeds from insurance?

Liability or Indemnity

☐ Is the liability clause mutual or is it tenant only?

☐ Is the landlord's liability limited to interest in the property?

Default

☐ Does the tenant have a cure period after notice of default?

☐ What remedies are available to the landlord for default?

Option to renew

☐ Does the tenant have the option to renew the lease?

☐ How long is the renewal option?

☐ How is rent determined for the renewal period?

☐ How much notice is required to exercise this option?

Right of first offer or right of first refusal for additional space

☐ Is there a right of first offer or first refusal on additional space in the building?

☐ How is rent for additional space determined?

☐ How long does the tenant have before exercising the right of first refusal or first offer?

Guaranty

☐ Is a personal guaranty required?

☐ When does the guaranty terminate?

Mortgages

☐ Can any mortgages adversely affect the tenant's rights if foreclosed upon?

Compliance with Law

☐ Does landlord warrant that the premises are in compliance with applicable law?

☐ If tenant is obligated to comply with applicable law, does it exclude matters that should more properly be the responsibility of the landlord, e.g., asbestos problems or disability access?

☐ Is landlord obligated to comply with all laws applicable to its control of the building?

Insurance

☐ What insurance is the tenant required to maintain?

☐ What insurance is the landlord required to maintain?

☐ Has your insurance agent reviewed the insurance requirements in the lease?

Rights of access

☐ Exclusive of emergencies, what notice must the landlord give in advance for entry into the tenant's premises?

☐ Are there any restrictions on the landlord interfering with tenant's business in showing the premises to buyers, lenders or prospective tenants?

Inspections

☐ Does the landlord have the right to enter and inspect the leased premises?

☐ If so, under what circumstances?

Signs

☐ Is the tenant allowed to put signage in or around the building and premises?

☐ What signage will the landlord provide, e.g., building monument, lobby listing, tenant's entry?

Parking

☐ How many parking spaces will be available for employees?

☐ Is there a cost for parking?

☐ Are there adequate spaces for visitors?

Holding Over

☐ Is the tenant allowed to remain in the space after the lease termination date?

☐ Is there an increase in rent during the hold-over period?

Quiet Enjoyment

☐ Does the landlord convey possession of the premises to the tenant through the quiet enjoyment clause?

Notices

☐ How are notices to be delivered?

☐ Is the contact information for both the landlord and the tenant included?

Rules and regulations for the building

☐ Are there specific rules and regulations in existence?

☐ Can the rules be changed without approval of tenant?

☐ Are there any rules that interfere with the expected operations of your business?

Lease Exhibits

☐ Confirm that all required lease exhibits are attached and accurate including:

- Site plan and property location description.

- Finalized space plan.

- Tenant improvement and construction schedule, if applicable.

If any additional changes are needed, redline the document and send to the landlord or landlord's agent for final review. Be sure that all exhibits are attached and accurate, including the space plan.

Executing the Lease

When the lease language has been finalized, the document is ready to be executed. Multiple copies of the lease and all exhibits, usually three or four, will be printed by the tenant, or delivered to the tenant for signature. More than one copy of the lease is signed by all parties so that each can retain a document with original signatures. The landlord, the tenant, and any brokerage firms involved in the transaction should each receive a fully executed original lease agreement.

The tenant is typically asked to sign the lease documents first. Documents signed by the tenant are then delivered to the landlord for signature. Plan to submit a check for any required deposits and first and/or last month's rent along with the signed documents.

Depending on the landlord's availability, it can take several days or longer before the lease is fully executed. It is important to note that the lease is not valid until it has been signed by both parties and the tenant should not consider the transaction complete until they are given an original lease document with all signatures.

10 | After the Lease is Signed

When the lease has been signed, depending on your timeline, the construction process should begin as soon as possible.

Tenant Improvements

The architect that prepared your space plan will now create a full-set of construction documents.

Construction documents or drawings are used for requesting a building permit and for the actual construction of your space. It is important that they are completely accurate and include everything you require. If something is left off of the final drawings, it may be difficult to have it added at a later date.

The final construction drawings will specify architectural walls and partitions. An electrical and communications distribution plan will precisely locate and relate components to appropriate office areas and workstations.

Ceiling plans will show locations of return ducts, ambient and architectural lighting, air diffusers and sprinkler heads; they will also describe the type and layout of the ceiling grid.

The landlord will typically employ a contractor to construct the tenant improvements and prepare the space for your occupancy.

Timeframes for tenant improvement projects can vary greatly depending on your geographic location and market conditions. Request timing estimates from the architect and contractor to confirm an approximate date when you can expect to move into the space.

After the Move

In the 30 to 60 days after your move, evaluate your premises and ensure everything meets expectations. Now is the time to bring any concerns you may have to the property manager or building owner.

Keep a record of these conversations, including the property manager's response and any actions taken. If the complaint is for something other than a minor issue, it is a good idea to put it in writing.

Summarizing Your Lease

As soon as possible after signing the lease, create a Lease Summary document, such as the example shown on the following page. A Lease Summary highlights the important features of your lease, enabling you to quickly locate the key terms you agreed to. The points you will want to include in the Lease Summary are usually the main issues from the lease proposal. Each item in the proposal will be expressed in layman's terms, which is appropriate for the Lease Summary.

Double check to insure that the layman's terms in the proposal correspond with the lease language and that the information is accurate.

Other items that should be included in the Lease Summary are the lease commencement and termination dates, the rental rate, the square footage of your space and the amount of your security deposit.

Lease Trigger Dates

Various options and rights in a lease may occur within a specific timeframe, such as 12-months after lease commencement, or within 60 days of the lease termination date. Keeping track of these lease trigger dates in your lease summary is an excellent way to make sure none of your hard-won "rights" slip through the cracks and are lost.

Lease Summary for The Easton Group

3180 Creekside Dr., Suite 209

Lease Term	5 years
Commencement Date	8/1/2016
Expiration Date	7/31/2021
Area	6,827 square feet

Rent Schedule

Year 1	$29.50	$201,396.50
Year 2	$30.00	$204,810.00
Year 3	$30.50	$208,223.50
Year 4	$31.00	$211,637.00
Year 5	$31.50	$215,050.50
Average Rent During Lease Term	**$30.50**	**$208,223.50**
Security Deposit	$16,783	
Services Included	Full Service - All Operating Expenses Included	

Critical Lease Information

Date	Clause	Explanation
Ongoing	Assignment/ Sublease	Tenant may sublease all or a portion of their leased premises, with the prior consent of the Landlord.
Ongoing	Right of First Refusal	Landlord will notify Tenant, as soon as possible, if there is a bona fide offer from a prospective tenant for any space adjacent to Tenant's leased premises. Tenant will have five business days to decide whether or not to accept the offer and acquire the additional space.

Date	Clause	Explanation
4/1/2021	Renewal Option	Tenant has the right to extend the lease for a term of 5 years, according to the same terms and conditions of the original lease, with the exception of the rental rate, which shall be at the then current market rate. Tenant must provide 120 days prior written notice of their intent to renew the lease. Landlord must respond within 10 business days with a proposed market rental rate for the renewal period. Tenant can either accept the proposed renewal rental rate, or must negotiate a mutually acceptable rate within 90 days of the expiration of the original lease term.
8/1/2021	Occupancy after Lease Expiration	Holdover after expiration of the lease will be at same rate paid immediately prior to lease expiration. Tenancy from month to month will be created, which may be terminated with 30 days written notice by either party.

Appendix A | Forms

The following pages contain templates for the forms referred to throughout this book.

As every leasing situation is unique, you may need to customize these forms to suit your particular circumstances.

Template forms include:

- Property Analysis

- Request for Proposal (RFP)

- Letter of Intent (LOI)

- Proposal Evaluation

- Proposal Summary

- Lease Summary

				PROPERTY ANALYSIS					
Location	Area/ Square Feet	Lease Term	Rental Rate/ Square Feet	Additional Expenses	Estimate of Additional Expenses**	Rental Rate w/ Expenses	Annual Cost of Occupancy	Growth Potential	Comments

Example Request for Proposal

Tenant Information:	
Premises:	
Area:	
Load Factor:	
Lease Commencement Date:	
Occupancy Date:	
Lease Term:	
Rental Rate:	
Security Deposit:	
Operating Expenses:	
Tenant Improvement Allowance:	
Option to Renew:	
Expansion Option:	

Space Planning:	
Assignment & Sublease:	
Signage:	
Access:	
Mechanical Systems:	
Fire/Safety Systems:	
Building Security:	
Elevators:	
Parking:	
Public Transportation:	
Additional Storage Space:	

Building Ownership:	
Property Management:	
Standard Lease:	
Building Amenities:	
Submittal Information:	

Proposal Evaluation

Proposal Items	Tenant's Request	Landlord's Response	Decision
Premises			
Area/Sq. Ft.			
Load Factor			
Lease Commencement Date			
Occupancy Date			
Lease Term			
Rental Rate			
Rent Escalation			
Security Deposit			
Operating Expenses			
Tenant Improvements			
Option to Renew			
Expansion Option			
Space Planning			
Assignment & Subleasing			
Signage			
Access			
Mechanical Systems			

Proposal Items	Tenant's Request	Landlord's Response	Decision
Fire/Safety Systems			
Building Security			
Elevators			
Public Transportation			
Parking			
Additional Storage Space			
Building Ownership			
Property Management			
Building Amenities			
Standard Lease			

Proposal Summary

Proposal Items	Proposal 1	Proposal 2	Proposal 3
Premises			
Area/Sq. Ft.			
Load Factor			
Lease Commencement Date			
Occupancy Date			
Lease Term			
Rental Rate			
Rent Escalation			
Security Deposit			
Operating Expenses			
Tenant Improvements			
Option to Renew			
Expansion Option			
Space Planning			
Assignment & Subleasing			
Signage			
Access			
Mechanical Systems			
Fire/Safety Systems			
Building Security			
Elevators			
Parking			

Proposal Items	Proposal 1	Proposal 2	Proposal 3
Public Transportation			
Additional Storage Space			
Building Ownership			
Property Management			
Building Amenities			
Standard Lease			
References			

Letter of Intent

This Letter of Intent is entered into for the purpose of stating the intent of all parties regarding space available for lease at 3180 Creekside Drive, Suite 210. Subject to the execution of a mutually acceptable Lease Agreement, this Letter of Intent will establish the basic terms and conditions for the Lease Agreement.

Landlord:	
Tenant:	
Location/Address:	
Use:	
Approximate Size:	
Lease Commencement Date:	
Occupancy Date:	
Lease Term:	
Rental Rate:	
Rent Escalation:	
Security Deposit:	
Tenant Improvements:	
Option to Renew:	

Expansion Option:	
Signage:	

The terms and conditions referenced above shall not be binding upon Landlord or Tenant until such time as the Lease and any related documents have been reviewed and approved by Tenant and Tenant's legal counsel and such Lease and documents have been fully executed by Landlord and Tenant.

Landlord: _____

Tenant: _____

Lease Summary	
Lease Term	
Commencement Date	
Expiration Date	
Area	

Rent Schedule		
Year 1		
Year 2		
Year 3		
Year 4		
Year 5		
Average Rent During Lease Term		
Security Deposit		
Services Included		

Critical Lease Information		
Date	**Clause**	**Explanation**

Appendix B | Example Lease

This lease document example is meant to provide a guideline for common and standard situations and should not be construed as specific legal advice for any specific situation. A commercial real estate professional or a real estate attorney can provide a lease document suited to your specific needs. For practical purposes, the following lease document example has been condensed.

COMMERCIAL LEASE AGREEMENT

THIS COMMERCIAL LEASE AGREEMENT ("Lease") is made and entered into by and between _____, a Limited Liability Company, hereinafter referred to as "Landlord" and _____, a Corporation, hereinafter referred to as "Tenant".

PREMISES. In consideration of the obligation of Tenant to make payments as herein provided and in consideration of the other terms, provisions and covenants hereof, Landlord hereby leases to Tenant and Tenant hereby leases from Landlord _____ square feet of rentable space, located at _____ ("Premises").

TERM. The Term shall be for 60 months ("Term"), commencing _____. The Term shall expire on _____.

BASE RENT. Tenant agrees to pay Landlord rent for each month hereof for said Premises the total sum of: $_____ per month. Monthly rent shall be due and payable on or before the first day of each calendar month during the Term. Said rents shall be past due on the tenth (10th) business day of each month. Any rent received after the tenth (10th) business day of each month, shall be subject to a late charge in an amount equal to 12 percent of such overdue amount.

SECURITY DEPOSIT. In addition, Tenant agrees to deposit with Landlord on commencement date a sum equal to one month of rent, which sum shall be held by Landlord, without obligation for interest, as security for the performance of Tenant's covenants and obligations under this Lease. If the Tenant fully performs the obligations under this Lease, the security deposit (or balance thereof) shall be returned to the Tenant within thirty (30) days after the Tenant vacates the Premises following the expiration of this Lease.

LATE CHARGE. Tenant agrees that monies paid to Landlord shall be applied first to any past due amounts including but not limited to rent, late charges, common area or other charges as provided for prior to applying monies to current charges. In the event Landlord has not received rent from Tenant by the close of the tenth (10th) day of the month, Tenant agrees to pay to Landlord on demand a late charge in accordance with the provisions of section 3, above.

RIGHT OF FIRST OFFER. Tenant shall have a right of first offer ("ROFO") during the initial Term of the Lease or any extension thereof with respect to office space contiguous to the Premises at the same terms and conditions contained in the Lease for the Premises. Landlord shall provide written notice to Tenant of the size and location of the available space. Tenant shall have 30 days to accept or reject the subject space. A rejection of space shall not constitute a waiver of Tenant's ROFO for subsequently available space.

OPTION TO RENEW. The Tenant shall have the option to renew the lease Term for one (1) renewal period, for a term of five (5) years commencing immediately following the expiration of the then current Term. The Annual Base Rent for the Premises shall be based on current market value.

ADDITIONAL RENT. Tenant shall pay to Landlord during each month of the Term hereof beginning in the second year of the Term, in addition to the Base Rent, Tenant's Share of increases in Operating Expenses incurred for the Building and the property common areas. Tenant shall not be responsible for any increases in Operating Expenses within Landlord's control in excess of five percent (5%) per year.

"Operating Expenses" are defined, for purposes of this Lease, as all costs incurred by Landlord relating to the ownership and operation of the building, and adjacent common areas including, but not limited to, the following:

The operation, repair and maintenance, in neat, clean, good order and condition, of the common areas, including parking areas, sidewalks, walkways, landscaped areas and fences.

The costs of water, gas, and electricity service.

- Trash disposal, property management and security services.
- Reserves set aside for maintenance and repair of the Premises.
- Taxes to be paid by Landlord for the Buildings and the

property.

- The cost of the premiums for the insurance policies maintained by Landlord.
- Any deductible portion of an insured loss concerning the Premises.

Tenant's share of any increases in the Operating Expenses shall be payable by Tenant monthly on the same day as the Base Rent is due hereunder. Landlord shall deliver to Tenant within sixty (60) days after the expiration of each calendar year a reasonably detailed statement ("Actual Statement") showing Tenant's Share of the actual increases in the Operating Expenses incurred during the preceding year. If Tenant's payments under this Paragraph during said preceding year exceed Tenant's Share as indicated on the Actual Statement, Landlord shall credit the amount of such overpayment against Tenant's Share of Operating Expenses next becoming due. If Tenant's payments under this Paragraph during said preceding year were less than Tenant's Share as indicated on the Actual Statement, Tenant shall pay to Landlord the amount of the deficiency within thirty (30) days after delivery by Landlord to Tenant of the Actual Statement.

USE OF THE PREMISES. Tenant shall use the Premises only for office purposes and for no other purpose without the written consent of Landlord.

TAXES. Landlord agrees to pay before they become delinquent all taxes (both general and special), assessments or governmental charges (hereinafter collectively referred to as "Taxes") lawfully levied or assessed against the Premises. Tenant shall pay all taxes, assessments, license fees and public charges levied upon its business operation, trade fixtures, leasehold improvements, merchandise and other personal property in or about the Premises.

INSURANCE. Tenant shall obtain and keep in force during the Term a Commercial General Liability policy of insurance in an amount of not less than $1,000,000 per occurrence protecting Tenant, Landlord and any Lender whose name has been provided to Tenant in writing (as Additional Insured / Managers or Landlords of Premises) against claims for bodily injury, personal injury and property damage based upon, involving or arising out of the ownership, use occupancy or maintenance of the Premises and all areas appurtenant thereto. Landlord shall obtain and keep in force during the Term a policy or policies in the name of Landlord with loss payable to Landlord and to any Lender insuring against loss or damage to the Premises.

LANDLORD'S REPAIRS AND MAINTENANCE. Landlord shall keep the common areas, roof, foundation, exterior walls, exterior glass, and all structural, mechanical, electrical, plumbing, fire/life/safety, HVAC, and any other systems and components of the Building (other than Tenant's improvements to the Premises), in good order, condition and repair, reasonable wear and tear excepted.

TENANT'S REPAIRS. Tenant shall repair any damage caused by the negligence of Tenant or Tenant's employees, agents or invitees, or caused by Tenant's default hereunder.

ALTERATIONS. Tenant shall not make any structural alterations, additions or improvements to the Premises without the prior written consent of Landlord. All shelves, machinery and trade fixtures installed by Tenant may be removed by Tenant at the termination of this Lease if Tenant so elects and shall be removed if required by Landlord.

SIGNS. Tenant shall not have the right to install any signage upon the exterior of the building. Tenant may install signage at the entry to the Tenant's Premises after first obtaining Landlord's approval as to design, materials, and size. Any signage shall be subject to any applicable governmental laws, ordinances, regulations and other requirements.

INSPECTIONS. Landlord and Landlord's agents and representatives shall have the right to enter and inspect the Premises at any time during reasonable business hours, for the purpose of ascertaining the condition of the Premises or in order to make such repairs as may be required to be made by Landlord under the terms of this Lease.

RIGHT OF ACCESS. Notwithstanding anything to the contrary contained in the Lease, all entries to the Premises shall be subject to the following conditions: (i) except in the case of any emergency, Landlord shall give Tenant reasonable prior notice, (ii) Landlord shall comply with Tenant's reasonable security requirements and procedures, (iii) all entries and all work performed by landlord during such entries shall be made and performed so as to minimize the extent and duration of any interference to Tenant's business.

UTILITIES. The Landlord shall provide heating, ventilation, and air conditioning services (HVAC) to the Premises at no charge to the Tenant. Such services shall be designed to maintain normal room temperatures from 8:00 a.m. to 8:00 p.m., Monday through Friday of each week and from 9:00 a.m. until 5:00 p.m. on Saturdays.

ASSIGNMENT AND SUBLETTING. Tenant shall have the right to assign this Lease or to sublet the whole or any part of the Premises with the prior written consent of Landlord, which shall not be unreasonably withheld, conditioned, or delayed.

DESTRUCTION AND CASUALTY DAMAGE. If the Building and/or the Premises should be damaged or destroyed by fire or other casualty, Landlord shall advise the Tenant within thirty (30) days of the destruction of Landlord's intent to repair or replace Building and Premises and Landlord's estimate of the time for completion of the repairs.

LIABILITY. Landlord shall not be liable to Tenant or Tenant's employees, agents, patrons, visitors or to any other person whomever, for any injury to person or damage to property on or about the Premises caused by the negligence or misconduct of anyone other than Landlord, its agents or employees. Tenant agrees to indemnify Landlord and hold it harmless from any loss, expense or claims, including attorney's fees, arising out of any such damage or injury.

PARKING. Tenant shall be entitled to its pro rata share of parking spaces based on a ratio of 4 spaces per 1,000 rentable square feet of space. Parking spaces throughout the entire parking area shall be shared by Landlord and all Tenants in the building.

CONDEMNATION. If the whole or any substantial part of the Premises should be taken for any public or quasi-public use under governmental law, ordinance or regulation, or by right of eminent domain, or by private purchase in lieu thereof, this Lease shall terminate and the rent shall be abated during the unexpired portion of this Lease, effective when the physical taking of said Premises shall occur.

HOLDING OVER. Should Tenant or any of its successors in interest, hold over the Premises or any part thereof, after the expiration of the Term, unless otherwise agreed in writing, such holding over shall constitute and be construed as tenancy from month-to-month.

QUIET ENJOYMENT. Landlord represents and warrants that it has full right and authority to enter into this Lease and that Tenant, upon paying the rental herein set forth and performing its other covenants and agreements herein set forth, shall peaceably and quietly have, hold and enjoy the Premises for the Term hereof without hindrance or molestation from Landlord, subject to terms and provisions of this Lease.

DEFAULT. The following events shall be deemed to be events of default by Tenant under this Lease:

> Tenant shall become insolvent or shall make a transfer in fraud to creditors or shall make an assignment for the benefit of creditors.

> Tenant shall file a petition under any section or chapter of the United States Bankruptcy Code, as amended, or under any similar law or statute of the United States or any State thereof; or Tenant shall be adjudged bankrupt or insolvent in proceedings filed against Tenant thereunder.

> A receiver or trustee shall be appointed for all or substantially all of the assets of Tenant.

> Tenant shall desert or vacate any substantial portion of the Premises.

REMEDIES. Upon the occurrence of any of such default described in DEFAULT paragraph hereof, Landlord shall have the option to terminate this Lease, in which event Tenant shall immediately surrender the Premises to Landlord.

NOTICES. Each provision of this instrument or of any applicable governmental laws, ordinances, regulations and other requirements with reference to the sending, mailing or delivery of any notice or the making of any payment by Landlord to Tenant or with reference to the sending, mailing delivery of any notice or the making of any payment by Tenant to Landlord shall be deemed to be complied with when and if the following steps are taken:

All rents and other payments required to be made by Tenant to Landlord hereunder shall be payable to Landlord at the address herein below set forth or at such other address as Landlord may specify from time to time by written notice delivered in accordance herewith.

All payments required to be made by Landlord to Tenant hereunder shall be payable to Tenant at the address herein below set forth or at such other address as Tenant may specify from time to time by written notice delivered in accordance herewith.

TENANT IMPROVEMENTS. Landlord shall provide Tenant with an improvement allowance in the amount of $15.00 per square foot.

MISCELLANEOUS. TIME IS OF THE ESSENCE OF THIS LEASE and all of the terms, provisions, covenants and conditions hereof.

The terms, provisions, covenants and conditions contained in this Lease shall apply to, and be binding upon the parties hereto and upon their respective heirs, legal representatives, successors and permitted assigns, except as otherwise herein expressly provided.

This Lease may not be altered, changed or amended except by an instrument in writing signed by Landlord and Tenant.

EXECUTED this _____ day of _____.

TENANT: _____

LANDLORD: _____

Appendix C | Glossary

Abatement
Commonly referred to as free rent or early occupancy and may occur outside or in addition to the primary term of the lease.

Absorption
The rate, expressed as a percentage, at which available space in the marketplace is leased during a predetermined period of time.

Actual Rent
Comprised of net rent plus operating expenses, and real estate taxes assessed on the building.

Ad Valorem
According to value. This is a tax imposed on the value of the property which is typically based on the local government's valuation of the property.

Add-On Factor
Often referred to as the Load Factor or Rentable/Usable (R/U) Factor, this represents the tenant's pro-rata share of the building common areas, such as lobbies, public corridors and restrooms. It is usually expressed as a percentage, which can then be applied to the usable square footage to determine the rentable square footage upon which the tenant will pay rent.

Anchor Tenant
The major or prime tenant in a shopping center, building, etc.

As-Is Condition
The acceptance by the tenant of the existing condition of the premises at the time the lease is consummated. This would include any physical defects.

Assignment
A transfer by lessee of lessee's entire estate in the property. Distinguishable from a sublease where the sublessee acquires something less than the lessee's entire interest.

Base Rent
A set amount used as a minimum rent in a lease with provisions for increasing the rent over the term of the lease.

Base Year
Actual taxes and operating expenses for a specified base year, most often the year in which the lease commences. Once the base year expenses are known, the lease essentially becomes a dollar stop lease. See also Dollar Stop.

Building Code
Local regulations that specify minimum structural requirements for design, construction, and materials used in a home or office building. Building codes are based on safety and health standards.

Building Standard
A list of construction materials and finishes that represent what the tenant improvement allowance is designed to cover while also serving to establish the landlord's minimum quality standards with respect to tenant finish improvements within the building. Examples of standard building items are: type and style of doors, lineal feet of partitions, quantity and quality of lighting, quality of floor coverings, wall coverings, etc.

Build-Out
The space improvements put in place per the tenant's specifications. Takes into consideration the amount of tenant improvement allowance provided for in the lease agreement.

Build-To-Suit
An approach taken to lease or sell space by a property owner where a new building is designed and constructed per the tenant's or buyer's specifications. The completed building is leased or sold to the tenant or buyer based upon a prior written agreement.

Certificate Of Occupancy
A document presented by a local government agency or building department certifying that the leased premises, have been satisfactorily inspected and are in a condition suitable for occupancy.

Clear-Span Facility
A building with vertical columns on the outside edges of the structure and a clear span between columns.

Common Area
Those areas within a building that are available for common use by all tenants or groups of tenants. Lobbies and public restrooms fall into this category.

Common Area Maintenance (CAM)
The amount of additional rent charged to a tenant, in addition to the base rent, to maintain the common areas of the property. Examples include: snow removal, outdoor lighting, parking lot maintenance, insurance, property taxes, etc.

Comparables
Lease rates and terms of properties similar in size, construction quality, age, use, and typically located within the same submarket and used as comparison properties to determine the fair market lease rate for another property with similar characteristics.

Concessions
Cash or cash equivalents extended by the landlord in the form of rental abatement, additional tenant improvement allowance, moving expenses, cabling expenses or other funds to influence or persuade a tenant to sign a lease.

Condemnation
The process of taking private property, without the consent of the owner, by a governmental agency for public use through the power of eminent domain. See also Eminent Domain.

Construction Management
The actual construction process is overseen by a qualified construction manager who ensures that the various stages of the construction process are completed in a timely and seamless fashion, from getting the construction permit to completion of the construction to the final walk-through.

Consumer Price Index (CPI)
Measures inflation in relation to the change in the price of a fixed market basket of goods and services purchased by a specified population during a "base" period of time. The CPI is commonly used to increase the base rental periodically as a means of protecting the landlord's rental stream against inflation.

Contiguous Space
Multiple suites/spaces within the same building and on the same floor, which can be combined and rented to a single tenant. Can also be a block of space located on multiple adjoining floors in a building (i.e., a tenant leases floors 6 through 8 in a building).

Contract Documents
The complete set of design plans and specifications for the construction of a building or of a building's interior improvements.

Conveyance
Most commonly refers to the transfer of title to property between parties by deed. The term may also include most of the instruments by which an interest in real estate is created, mortgaged or assigned.

Deed
A legal instrument transferring title to real property from the seller to the buyer upon the sale of such property.

Default
The general failure to perform a legal or contractual duty or to discharge an obligation when due. Some specific examples are: (1) Failure to make a payment of rent when due. (2) The breach or failure to perform any of the terms of a lease agreement.

Demising Wall
The partition wall that separates one tenant's space from another or from the building's common area such as a public corridor.

Depreciation
Spreading out the cost of a capital asset over its estimated useful life or a decrease in the usefulness, and therefore value, of real property improvements or other assets caused by deterioration or obsolescence.

Dollar Stop
An agreed dollar amount of taxes and operating expense (expressed for the building as a whole or on a square foot basis) over which the tenant will pay its prorated share of increases.

Eminent Domain
A power of the state, municipalities, and private persons or corporations authorized to exercise functions of public character to acquire private property for public use by condemnation, in return for just compensation.

Environmental Impact Statement
Documents which are required by federal and state laws to accompany proposals for major projects and programs that will likely have an impact on the surrounding environment.

Escalation Clause
A clause in a lease which provides for the rent to be increased to reflect changes in expenses paid by the landlord such as real estate taxes, operating costs, etc. This may

be accomplished by several means such as fixed periodic increases, increases tied to the Consumer Price Index or adjustments based on changes in expenses paid by the landlord in relation to a dollar stop or base year reference.

Estoppel Certificate
A signed statement certifying that certain facts are correct as of the date of the statement and can be relied upon by a third party, including a prospective lender or purchaser.

Expense Stop
An agreed dollar amount of taxes and operating expense (expressed for the building as a whole or on a square foot basis) over which the tenant will pay its prorated share of increases.

Face Rental Rate
The asking rental rate for a building or specific office space published by the landlord.

First Generation Space
Generally refers to new space that is currently available for lease and has never before been occupied by a tenant.

Fixed Costs
Costs, such as rent, which do not fluctuate in proportion to the level of sales or production.

Flex Space
A building that provides its occupants flexibility in how they utilize the space. Configurations usually allow a flexible amount of office or showroom space in combination with manufacturing, laboratory, warehouse distribution, etc. Typically also provides the flexibility to relocate overhead doors. Flex space is generally constructed with load-bearing floors, loading dock facilities, high ceilings and few or no common areas.

Force Majeure
A force that cannot be controlled by the parties to a contract and prevents said parties from complying with the provisions of the contract. This includes acts of God such as a flood or a hurricane or, acts of man such as a strike, fire or war.

Full Service
An all-inclusive rental rate that includes operating expenses and real estate taxes for the first year (base year). The tenant is generally still responsible for any increase in operating expenses over the base year amount. See also Base Year.

Future Proposed Space

Space in a proposed commercial development which is not yet under construction or where no construction start date has been set. Future proposed projects include all those projects waiting for an anchor tenant, financing, zoning, approvals or any other event necessary to begin construction. Also may refer to the future phases of a multi-phase project.

General Contractor

The prime contractor who contracts for the construction of an entire building or project, rather than just a portion of the work. The general contractor hires subcontractors, (e.g., plumbing, electrical, etc.), coordinates all work, and is responsible for payment to subcontractors.

General Partner

A member of a partnership who has authority to bind the partnership. A general partner also shares in the profits and losses of the partnership. See also Limited Partnership.

Graduated Lease

A lease, generally long-term in nature, which provides that the rent will vary depending upon future contingencies, such as a periodic appraisal, the tenant's gross income or simply the passage of time.

Gross Building Area

The total floor area of the building measuring from the outer surface of exterior walls and windows and including elevator shafts, stairwells, atriums and basement space.

Gross Lease

A lease in which the tenant pays a flat sum for rent out of which the landlord must pay all expenses such as taxes, insurance, maintenance, utilities, etc.

Ground Rent

Rent paid to the owner for use of land, normally on which to build a building. Generally, the arrangement is that of a long-term lease (e.g. 99 years) with the lessor retaining title to the land.

High-Rise

In a downtown submarket, high-rise refers to a building higher than 25 stories above ground level, but in suburban submarkets, it generally refers to buildings higher than 7 or 8 stories.

Hold Over Tenant

A tenant retaining possession of the leased premises after the expiration of a lease.

HVAC
The acronym for Heating, Ventilating and Air-Conditioning.

Improvements
In the context of leasing, this term typically refers to the improvements made to a building but may include any permanent structure or other development, such as a street, sidewalks, utilities, etc. See also Leasehold Improvements and Tenant Improvements.

Indirect Costs
Development costs other than material and labor costs, which are directly related to the construction of improvements, including administrative and office expenses, commissions, architectural, engineering and financing costs.

Landlord's Lien or Warrant
A warrant from a landlord to levy upon a tenant's personal property (e.g., furniture, etc.) and to sell this property at a public sale to compel payment of the rent or the observance of some other stipulation in the lease.

Lease
An agreement whereby the owner of real property (landlord/lessor) gives the right of possession to another (tenant/lessee) for a specified period of time (term) and for a specified consideration (rent).

Lease Agreement
The formal legal document entered into between a landlord and a tenant to reflect the terms of the negotiations between them; that is, the lease terms have been negotiated and agreed upon, and the agreement is in writing.

Leasehold Improvements
Improvements made to the leased premises by or for a tenant. Generally part of the negotiations will include in some detail the improvements to be made in the leased premises by the landlord. See also Tenant Improvements.

LEED
Leadership in Energy and Environmental Design (LEED) is a green building certification system, providing third-party verification that a building was designed and built using strategies to improve energy efficiency, and reduce CO_2 emissions.

Legal Description
A geographical description identifying a parcel of land by government survey or lot numbers of a recorded plat.

Letter of Attornment
A letter from the grantor to a tenant, stating that a property has been sold, and directing rent to be paid to the grantee (buyer).

Letter of Credit
A commitment by a bank or other person, made at the request of a customer, that the issuer will honor drafts or other demands for payment upon full compliance with the conditions specified in the letter of credit.

Letter of Intent
A preliminary agreement stating the proposed terms for a final contract. They can be binding or non-binding. The parties should always consult their respective legal counsel before signing any Letter of Intent.

Limited Partnership
A type of partnership, created under state law, comprised of one or more general partners who manage the business and who are personally liable for partnership debts, and one or more special or limited partners who contribute capital and share in profits but who take no part in running the business and incur no liability over and above the amount contributed. See also General Partner.

Low Rise
A building with fewer than 4 stories above ground level.

Market Rent
The rental income that a property would command on the open market with a landlord and a tenant ready and willing to consummate a lease in the ordinary course of business; indicated by the rents that landlords were willing to accept and tenants were willing to pay in recent lease transactions for comparable space.

Market Value
The highest price a property would command in a competitive and open market under all conditions requisite to a fair sale with the buyer and seller each acting prudently and knowledgeably in the ordinary course of trade.

Master Lease
A primary lease that controls subsequent leases.

Mechanic's Lien
A claim created by state statutes for the purpose of securing priority of payment of the price and value of work performed and materials furnished in constructing, repairing or improving a building or other structure, and which attaches to the land as well as to the buildings and improvements thereon.

Metes and Bounds
The boundary lines of land, with their terminal points and angles, described by listing the compass directions and distances of the boundaries.

Mid-Rise
A building with between four and eight stories above ground level although in a downtown submarket, this may extend to buildings up to twenty-five stories high.

Mixed-Use
Space within a building or project providing for more than one use (i.e., a loft or apartment project with retail, an apartment building with office space, an office building with retail space).

Net Lease
A lease in which there is a provision for the tenant to pay, in addition to rent, certain costs associated with the operation of the property. These costs may include property taxes, insurance, repairs, utilities, and maintenance. There are also double net (NN) and triple net (NNN) leases. The difference between the three is the degree to which the tenant is responsible for operating costs.

Non-Compete Clause
A clause that can be inserted into a lease specifying that the business of the tenant is exclusive in the property and that no other tenant operating the same or similar type of business can occupy space in the building. This clause benefits service-oriented businesses desiring exclusive access to the building's population (i.e. stock brokerage firm, travel agency, bank, etc.).

Normal Wear and Tear
The deterioration or loss in value caused by the tenant's normal and reasonable use. In many leases the tenant is not responsible for normal wear and tear.

Operating Expenses
The actual costs associated with operating a property including maintenance, repairs, management, utilities, taxes and insurance.

Operating Expense Escalation
Although there are many variations of escalation clauses, all are intended to adjust rents by reference to external standards such as published indexes, negotiated wage levels, or actual expenses related to the ownership and operation of the building. During the past thirty years, landlords have developed the custom of separating the base rent for the occupancy of the leased premises from escalation rent. This technique enables the landlord to better ensure that the net rent to be received under the lease will not be reduced by the normal costs of operating and maintaining the property.

Parking Ratio or Index
The amount of parking available to a building expressed as the quantity of spaces per 1,000 square feet of rentable space.

Pass Through Expenses
A tenant's pro rata share of operating expenses (i.e. taxes, utilities, repairs) paid in addition to the base rent.

Percentage Lease
Often found in retail leases, a percentage lease refers to a provision calling for the landlord to be paid a percentage of the tenant's gross sales as a component of rent. There is usually a base rent amount to which a percentage rent is then added.

Personal Guaranty
A personal guaranty is a contract between you and the landlord that obligates you personally to fulfill the financial terms of the lease in the event of default.

Preleased
Space in a proposed building that has been leased before the start of construction or during construction.

Punch List
An itemized list, typically prepared by the architect or construction manager, documenting incomplete or unsatisfactory items after the contractor has notified the owner that the tenant space is substantially complete.

Quiet Enjoyment
Quiet enjoyment, also referred to as warranty of possession, provides a warranty by the landlord that he or she has the legal ability to convey the possession of the premises to tenant. This is the essence of the landlord's agreement and the tenant's obligation to pay rent.

Raw Land
Unimproved land that remains in its natural state.

Raw Space
Unimproved shell space in a building.

Rehab
An extensive renovation of a building or project which is intended to provide an updated look and feel to a commercial building.

Renewal Option
A clause giving a tenant the right to extend the term of a lease, usually for a stated period of time and at a rent amount as provided for in the option language.

Rent
Compensation or fee paid, usually periodically, for the occupancy and use of any rental property, land, buildings, equipment, etc.

Rent Commencement Date
The date on which a tenant begins paying rent. The dynamics of the marketplace will dictate whether this date coincides with the lease commencement date or if it commences months later (i.e., in a weak market, the tenant may be granted several months free rent).

Rentable Square Footage
The usable square footage plus the tenant's pro rata share of the building common areas, such as lobbies, public corridors and restrooms.

Rentable/Usable Ratio
The number obtained when the Total Rentable Area in a building is divided by the Usable Area in the building. The inverse of this ratio describes the proportion of space that an occupant can expect to actually utilize and/or physically occupy.

Rent-Up Period
That period of time, following construction of a new building, when tenants are actively being sought and the project is approaching its stabilized occupancy.

Request For Proposal (RFP)
The formalized Request for Proposal represents a compilation of the considerations that a tenant might have and should be customized to reflect their specific needs. Just as the building's standard form lease document represents the landlord's wish list, the RFP is the tenant's wish list.

Right of First Refusal
A lease clause giving a tenant the first opportunity to lease additional space that may become available in a property at the same price and on the same terms and conditions as those contained in a third-party offer that the owner has expressed a willingness to accept. This right is often restricted to specific areas of the building such as adjacent suites or other suites on the same floor.

Second Generation
Refers to previously occupied space that becomes available for lease, either directly from the landlord or as sublease space. See also First Generation Space.

Security Deposit
A deposit of money by a tenant to a landlord to secure performance of a lease.

Shell Space
Unfinished office space.

Site Development

The installation of all necessary improvements, (i.e. installment of utilities, grading, etc.), made to a site before a building or project can be constructed upon such site.

Site Plan

A detailed plan which depicts the location of improvements on a parcel of land which also contains all the information required by the zoning ordinance.

Space Plan

A graphic representation of a tenant's space requirements, showing wall and door locations, room sizes, outlet locations, etc. A preliminary space plan will be prepared for a prospective tenant at any number of different properties and this serves as a "test-fit" to help the tenant determine which property will best meet its requirements. When the tenant has selected a building of choice, a final space plan is prepared which speaks to all of the landlord and tenant objectives and is then approved by both parties. It must be sufficiently detailed to allow an accurate estimate of the construction costs. This final space plan will become an exhibit to any lease negotiated between the parties.

Specific Performance

A requirement compelling one of the parties to perform or carry out the provisions of a contract into which he has entered.

Speculative Space

Any tenant space that has not been leased before the start of construction on a new building.

Step-Up Lease

A lease that provides for a lower rental amount paid at the beginning of the tenancy and greater amount paid toward the end of the tenancy. This rental rate method works well for companies that plan to grow their revenues over the term of the lease and want to pay the lowest rent available during the first few months or years of the lease term.

Subcontractor

A contractor working under and being paid by the general contractor. Often a specialist, such as an electrical contractor, cement contractor, etc.

Subordination Agreement

As used in a lease, the tenant generally accepts the leased premises subject to any recorded mortgage or deed of trust lien and all existing recorded restrictions, and the landlord is often given the power to subordinate the tenant's interest to any first mortgage or deed of trust lien subsequently placed upon the leased premises.

Survey
The process by which a parcel of land is measured and its boundaries and contents determined and specified.

Tenant
One who rents real estate from another and holds an estate by virtue of a lease.

Tenant Representative
A commercial real estate agent who specializes in representing the interests of tenants.

Tenant at Will
When a tenant occupies property with the consent of the landlord, but without an agreement that specifies the rental terms.

Tenant Improvements
Improvements made to the leased premises by or for a tenant. Generally, lease negotiations will include the improvements to be made in the leased premises by the landlord. See also Leasehold Improvements.

Tenant Improvement Allowance
Defines the fixed amount of money contributed by the landlord toward tenant improvements. The tenant pays any of the costs that exceed this amount.

Trade Fixtures
Personal property that is attached to a structure (e.g., shelving attached to the walls of the leased premises) used in the tenant's business. Since this property is part of the business and not deemed to be part of the real estate, it is typically removable by the tenant upon lease termination.

Triple Net (NNN) Rent
A lease in which the tenant pays, in addition to rent, certain costs associated with a leased property, which may include property taxes, insurance premiums, repairs, utilities, and maintenances. There are also net leases and double net (NN) leases, depending upon the degree to which the tenant is responsible for operating costs.

Turn-Key Project
The construction of a project in which a third party, usually a developer or general contractor, is responsible for the total completion of a building (including construction and interior design) or, the construction of tenant improvements to the customized requirements and specifications of a future owner or tenant.

Use
The specific purpose for which a parcel of land or a building is intended to be used or for which it has been designed or arranged.

Usable Square Footage
The area contained within the demising walls of the tenant space.

Vacancy Rate
The total amount of available space compared to the total inventory of space, expressed as a percentage.

Vacant Space
Existing tenant space currently being marketed for lease.

Variance
Permission that allows a property owner to depart from the literal requirements of a zoning ordinance that, because of special circumstances, cause a unique hardship.

Warranty Of Possession
Another term for the quiet enjoyment clause providing a warranty by the landlord that he or she has the legal ability to convey the possession of the premises to a tenant. This is the essence of the landlord's agreement and the tenant's obligation to pay rent.

Workletter
A list of the building standard items that the landlord will contribute as part of the tenant improvements. Examples of the building standard items typically identified include: style and type of doors, lineal feet of partitions, type and quantity of lights, quality of floor coverings, number of telephone and electrical outlets, etc. See also Leasehold Improvements and Tenant Improvements.

Working Drawings
The set of plans for a building or office space that comprise the contract documents that indicate the precise manner in which a project is to be built. This set of plans includes a set of specifications for the building or office space.

Zoning
The division of a city or town into zones and the application of regulations having to do with the structural, architectural design and intended use of buildings within such designated zone.

Zoning Ordinance
The set of laws and regulations, generally, at the city or county level, controlling the use of land and construction of improvements in a given area or zone.

Index

Karen Warner is an office relocation specialist and commercial real estate broker. She has helped hundreds of companies with their relocation objectives. In addition to *Winning the Office Leasing Game*, Karen is also the author of *Office Relocation Planner* and *Move Your Office*. Her extensive knowledge of the commercial relocation process and unique talent as a tenant representative has helped many businesses manage a smooth transition to their new location.

www.ingramcontent.com/pod-product-compliance
Lightning Source LLC
Chambersburg PA
CBHW051348200326
41521CB00014B/2514